School in a desert

Diana and Mohamed Al Mawed

Contents

1	The emirate of Dubai	2
2	The people of the Arabian Desert	4
3	How a desert is formed	5
4	Desert oil-fields	7
5	The seasons and the weather	8
6	The position of the school	12
7	How the children get to school	14
8	The design of the school	15
9	The Arabic language	18
10	The school day and the school year	21
11	What the children eat	24
12	Out of school activities	26
13	Festivals	28
14	School outings	30
	Glossary	31
	Further information	32
	Index	33

1 The Emirate of Dubai

Dubai is a small Arab state in the Middle East. It lies between the waters of the Arabian Gulf and the great Arabian Desert. It is rich and important because it has oil.

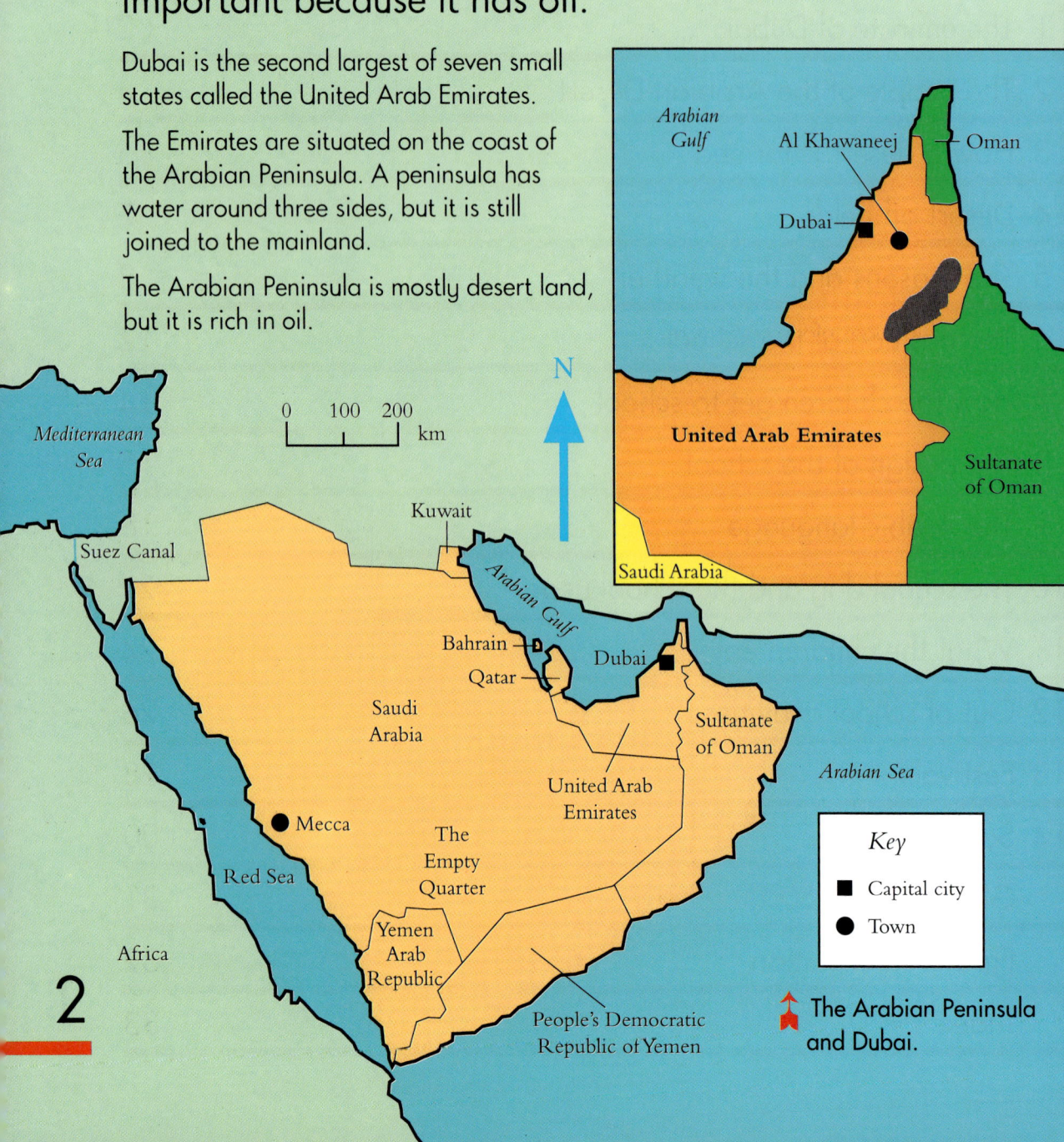

Dubai is the second largest of seven small states called the United Arab Emirates.

The Emirates are situated on the coast of the Arabian Peninsula. A peninsula has water around three sides, but it is still joined to the mainland.

The Arabian Peninsula is mostly desert land, but it is rich in oil.

The Arabian Peninsula and Dubai.

↑ Trading boats called dhows load and unload their goods along Dubai Creek.

Dubai
The Emirate and City

Dubai is made up of about 3900 square kilometres of flat desert, with 70 kilometres of coastline. Most of the population of 528,000 live in the city of Dubai.

Not long ago Dubai was just a small port for trading, fishing and pearl-diving. Now, because of the oil money, it has become a busy, international city with first-class hotels, expensive shopping centres, and green parks. People from all over the world work in Dubai.

Dubai is built on either side of Dubai Creek. A creek is an inlet of water coming in from the sea.

Travelling to the village

Wide tree-lined roads lead out of the city across the sandy desert. They go past built-up village suburbs, large villas, and farms irrigated with water from underground wells. Twenty kilometres to the east of the city, there is a small desert village called Al Khawaneej.

This book is about life in the desert and in the Girls' School in Al Khawaneej.

↑ The village of Al Khawaneej.

2 The people of the Arabian Desert

The people who live in the Arabian Desert are called Bedu. The Bedu are traditionally nomadic, which means that they do not live in one place, but move from place to place. However, some of them now live in towns and villages.

The Bedu travel across the desert sand with their animals, moving from one watering place to another according to the season. They stop where there is an oasis or some grazing land. Their homes are large tents made from goats' hair.

The people of Al Khawaneej are Bedu, but they are no longer nomadic. Deep wells have been drilled into the ground in Al Khawaneej to supply water for irrigating the desert land. Now there are green farms where once there was only sand. The farmers grow date, almond and lime trees, as well as vegetables such as aubergines and cauliflowers.

Most families still keep camels, but nowadays they use four-wheel drive cars to travel across the sand.

⬆ The Bedu who live in the desert travel by camel. A camel can live for many days without water. It is called the ship of the desert.

⬅ The Bedu of Al Khawaneej have settled in the village in modern houses with water and electricity.

3 How a desert is formed

There are large parts of the world where it hardly ever rains. The ground is mostly dry sand or rock, and not many plants grow there. These places are called deserts. It is very hot in most deserts.

Millions of years ago many of the world's deserts were beneath the sea. As time went by, movement inside the earth's crust pushed the land up out of the sea. Later the sea dried up. Large areas of dry sand and rock were left as desert lands.

You can still find shells and fossils in deserts.

↑ A fossilised fish.

↑ Al Khawaneej is surrounded by desert sand.

⬆ One third of the Arabian Peninsula is sand

An oasis is a place in the desert where there is fresh water.

Desert landscapes

Desert scenery can be quite varied. Some parts are flat areas of hard sand or gravel. In other places the wind blows the loose sand into high hills called dunes. Some dunes have sharp ridges along the top. Much of the desert is rocky or mountainous.

The southern part of the Arabian Desert is all sand. Some of the dunes are a hundred kilometres long, and it is so hot that no one dares to cross this part in the summer months. It is known as The Empty Quarter.

In some places in the desert there is water just below the ground. Trees and plants grow naturally there, and people can dig wells to get fresh water. A place like this is called an oasis. An oasis is often in a low place like a valley. Sometimes an oasis has enough water for a large town to be built there.

6

4 Desert oil fields

At night, far beyond Al Khawaneej Girls' School, you can see a bright flame. It is a petroleum gas flare.

Many of the world's oilfields lie either below sea beds or below the desert sands. Millions of years ago tiny animals and plants died and sank to the bottom of the sea. Thick layers of mud covered them.

Over a long period of time, the mud turned into soft rock. As the animals and plants rotted away, the weight of the rocks above and the heat of the earth below turned the remains into oil and gas.

As time went by, hard rocks formed above the soft rocks, trapping the oil below. Later some of the seas dried up. The oil was then under the desert sand.

The petroleum in the ground is called crude oil. By refining crude oil, we get other types of oil such as petrol, diesel, and oil for heating homes. Petrol in Dubai is not expensive.

Many household goods are made from the chemicals in petroleum. Some of these are manufactured in Dubai, like plastic and paint.

The United Arab Emirates produce about 4 per cent of the world's oil.

5 The seasons and the weather

Dubai has two seasons. There is a long, very hot summer, and there is a cooler winter season.

Summer starts at the end of April and lasts until October. As Dubai is on the coast, the weather there is very sticky and humid. Away from the sea the desert air is dry. July and August are the hottest months.

In October it starts to get cooler, and it remains pleasant until April. In the winter there is a little rain, and this flows into underground wells. There are sometimes strong winds and sandstorms.

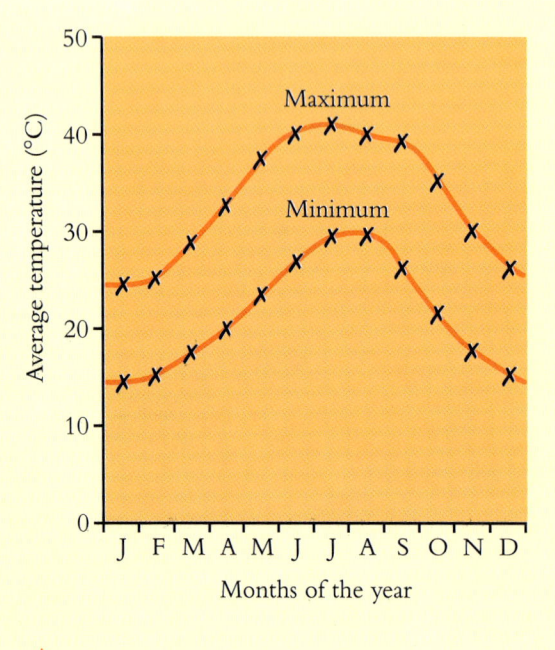

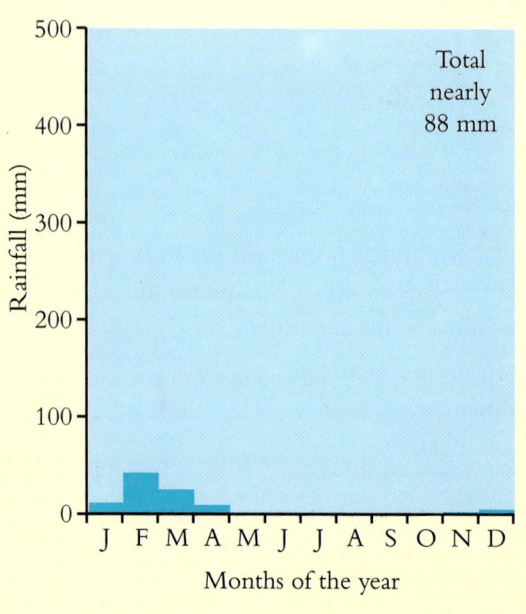

↑ Graph showing average temperatures in Dubai.

↑ Bar chart showing rainfall in Dubai. Total nearly 88 mm

↑ Children **play** in celebration of the rain after a hot, dry period.

↑ An evening barbecue.

The Summer

In the summer children play outside only in the early morning and in the evening, when it is cooler. The rest of the day they spend indoors, where the air-conditioning is kept on full. They drink plenty of water to help them to keep cool.

In the middle of summer the desert sand is too hot to walk on, and the hot air wavers above the ground. Sometimes a thirsty desert traveller thinks that he sees water rippling in the distance, but when he reaches the place, he finds only sand. This is called a mirage. The water that he thinks he sees is really only the blue sky reflected in the hot air waves.

The Winter

When the winter season starts in October, children enjoy evening picnics in the cool desert air.

At night-time the desert air can be very cold, because there are no clouds to keep the heat near the earth.

Winter is also the time for rainstorms and sandstorms.

After the winter rains there is water in the wadis and everything is green.

Rainstorms

A desert is a place where the rainfall is less than 250mm a year. Dubai has about 88mm a year.

Life in the desert depends upon the winter rainfall to fill the oases, the underground well-fields, and the dry river-beds known as wadis. In Dubai special prayers are said for rain.

In Dubai it rains mostly between January and March. Even then, there is rain on only a few days each month. A winter rainstorm can be sudden and violent. The dry wadis fill up with fast-moving water which runs down from the hills – anything in its path may be swept away.

After a rainstorm the desert sand turns green, and small, brightly-coloured flowers spring up from the previous year's seeds. They bloom for just a few weeks.

In the villages, wells are dug to a depth of at least 60 metres, and the water is pumped to ground level and used to irrigate the farms. It may take years for the rain which falls on higher ground to flow underground and to reach the well-fields.

The farms in Al Khawaneej are irrigated by a system of small straight channels cut into the sandy ground.

Sandstorms

In the winter months strong winds from the north-west blow across the Arabian Gulf, causing sandstorms in Dubai. The loose desert sand is blown up into the air. Motorists slow down as sand swirls everywhere. Winds blowing across the desert can even change the shape of the sand dunes.

A sandstorm usually lasts for several hours. When the wind drops, everything settles down again, leaving the inside of homes and schools covered with dust. Extra cleaning must be done before the next sandstorm blows up.

⬆ People have to protect their faces during a sandstorm.

6 The position of the school

There is a main road into Al Khawaneej, but no road out of it. Beyond the village there is the desert. On the sand at the end of the village stands the Girls' School.

Most of the village is made up of large farms owned by landowners from Dubai. Some of the Bedu families live in simple Arab-style houses near the school. Others live just outside the village.

Close to the school there are two shops, a small grocery shop and a clothes shop. There is also a small mosque. A mosque is a holy place where Muslim men pray. Muslim women usually pray at home.

⬆ The farmers near the school grow dates and a kind of grass for animals to eat, called barseem.

⬆ Most Arab houses have a courtyard in the middle. This is a safe place for children to play.

Around the school

There are no tarmac roads beyond the Girls' School – only jeep tracks. You need a four-wheel drive car to go any further. The tracks lead across the sand dunes, past animal pens with cows, bulls and goats in them. They lead to a camel track. This is used for training racing-camels. Camel-racing is a serious sport in Dubai.

Most of the Bedu men in Al Khawaneej work as camel trainers on the farms. Others work as personal guards to the Sheikhs in Dubai. Sheikhs are men from the ruling family.

Many of the fathers of the girls attending the Girls' School also have their own camels, which they train in the afternoons. The young Al Khawaneej boys accompany their fathers at weekends and during the holidays to learn the camel profession. The Bedu traditions are very strong amongst the Al Khawaneej families.

Many of the best racing camels in Dubai come from Al Khawaneej.

Jeep tracks lead over the sand by the Girls' School to the camel farms in the dunes.

7 How the children get to school

Most children in Dubai go to school by school bus or by car. Young children are not allowed to walk or cycle to school.

⬆ The three girls' buses in Al Khawaneej take the girls to school in the morning.

Dubai has many modern primary schools, but Al Khawaneej needs only one school for boys and one for girls.

The boys wait for their school bus near the grocery shop. The girls' buses stop at each girl's house in turn.

At lunch-time the buses take the girls in Grades 1, 2 and 3 home first, and then return for the older girls, who have an extra lesson at the end of the morning.

The bus journeys are free. Children in Dubai do not pay for anything at school.

⬆ Some children in Al Khawaneej go to school by car with the family's driver.

8 The design of the school

The Girls' School is shaped like many Arab houses. It has rooms on the ground floor only, and a flat roof. There is a high wall round the outside, and a large square courtyard in the middle.

Tall trees planted against the outside wall make good sand-barriers.

The rooms in the Girls' School form a square. The courtyard in the middle is very useful because it is private and sheltered. (All Arab houses have a private area like this.)

In the corners of the courtyard there are benches under shady almond trees. At one end of the courtyard there is a flagpole. The flag of the United Arab Emirates flies there: it is red, green, black and white.

The school courtyard is used for assembly, break-time and sports.

There are 210 pupils aged from 6 to 18 in Al Khawaneej Girls' School. 130 of the pupils are in the primary section.

There are six classrooms for the primary school pupils, one for each Grade, and these lie along one side of the courtyard.

At the back of the school there are volleyball and basketball courts for winter play, and a large hall which is used for concerts and dancing displays.

At the front of the school there are offices for the headmistress and for the teachers, a library, a music room and a first aid room.

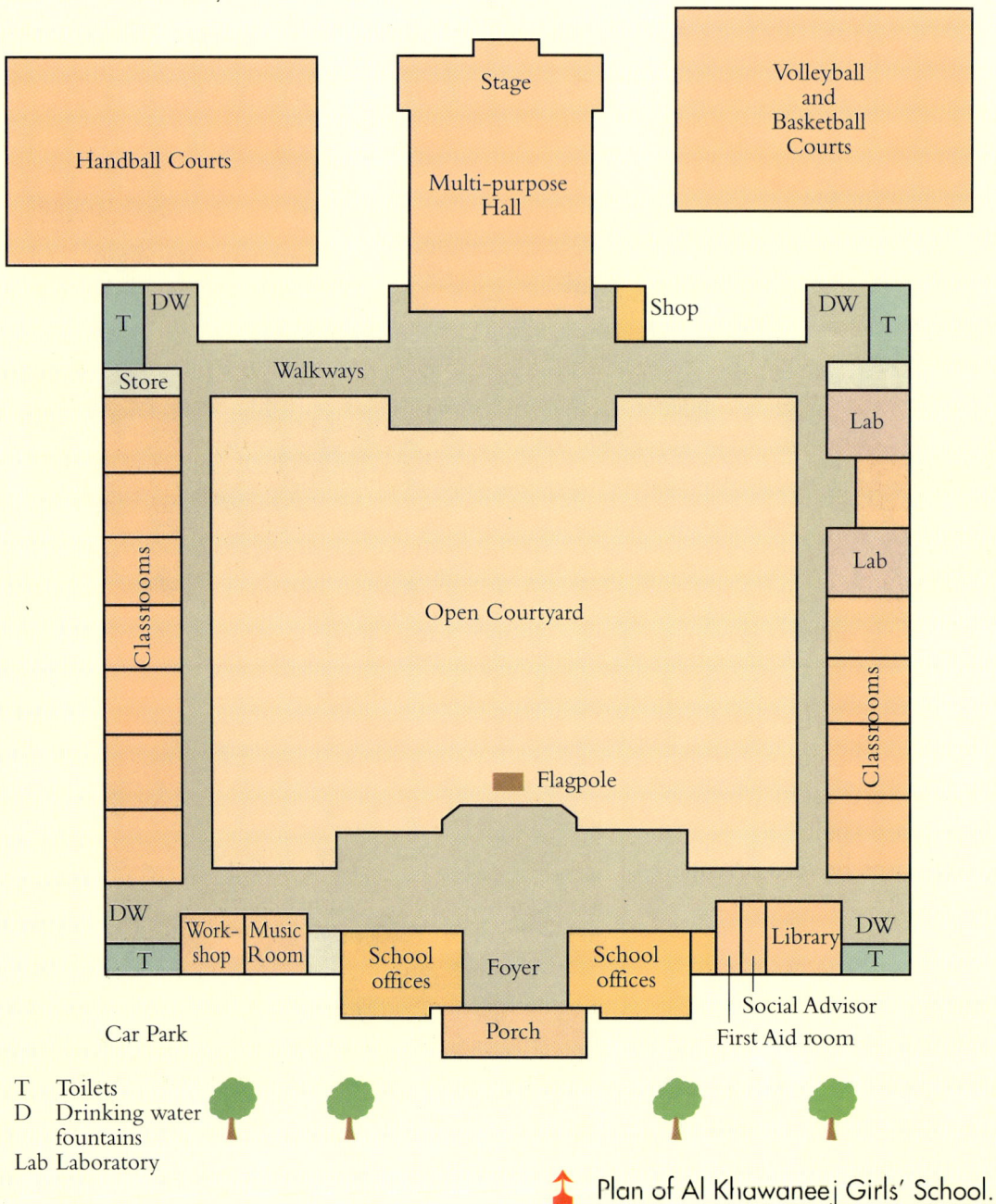

Handball Courts

Stage
Multi-purpose Hall

Volleyball and Basketball Courts

DW
T
Store
Walkways
Shop
DW
T
Lab
Classrooms
Lab
Open Courtyard
Classrooms
Flagpole
DW
T
Work-shop
Music Room
School offices
Foyer
School offices
Library
DW
T
Social Advisor
First Aid room
Car Park
Porch

T   Toilets
D   Drinking water fountains
Lab Laboratory

Plan of Al Khawaneej Girls' School.

↑ The walkways.

Keeping cool and drinking water

In a desert climate children need to keep cool. Cloisters round the courtyard inside the Girls' School provide cool and breezy places to walk, and the classrooms have electric fans and air-conditioning.

The pupils are always thirsty, so there are drinking fountains in each corner of the school. In Al Khawaneej the water is pumped up from deep wells, and then it is filtered so that it does not taste salty.

When the children visit the city, they drink desalinated sea-water. Desalination is a process which turns salty water into clean drinking water. The sea-water evaporates into steam, and the steam then condenses back into water. The condensed water has no salt left in it.

The pupils can also buy bottled mineral water which comes from mountain springs in the United Arab Emirates.

9 The Arabic language

The pupils at Al Khawaneej Girls' School speak Arabic.

Books in Arabic start at what we think of as the back of the book. The beginning of an Arabic book is where English and other Western-language books end.

Arabic writing goes across the page from right to left.

Arabic writing is always joined up. Pupils at Al Khawaneej Girls' School learn to join up their letters right from Grade 1.

There are 28 letters in the Arabic alphabet. There are no capital letters, but each letter has a slightly different shape if it is at the beginning, in the middle, or at the end of a word.

Pupils in Grades 1 and 2 use slates to practise writing from right to left. ➡➡

Long ago the Arabs brought their way of writing numbers to Europe. Most of the numbers we use today come from the Arabic ones.

Learning Arabic and English

In Dubai both Arabic and English are spoken. Arabic is the official language of the country, but English is used amongst all the different nationalities living there.

There are both Arabic and English channels on television, and the pupils at Al Khawaneej Girls' School start to learn English in Grade 1.

▲ All signs and stamps in Dubai are written both in Arabic and in English.

◄ There are 100 fils in one dirham.

Some pupils learning both Arabic and English at the same time have difficulties learning the differences between the two languages.

■ In Arabic the comma, tick and question mark are the other way round.

■ Arabic does not have the letters p, v, g, o or e. Arab children find it very difficult to pronounce 'p'. Arabic has several letters which are not in the English alphabet. One of these is the 'kh' in Al Khawaneej; it sounds like the Scottish 'ch' in 'loch'.

■ The vowels a, i and u are written as signs above and below the previous letter. Children learn these signs, but in books and newspapers they are usually left out.

■ Arabic and English are written in opposite directions. Sometimes children become confused and write some letters back to front.

▲ Arabic letters are always pronounced in the same way, so children learn to read quite quickly.

19

Muslims always face towards Mecca when they pray. Before entering the mosque, they remove their shoes.

Arabic and Islam

Arabic was first spoken in the Arabian Peninsula. During the seventh century the first Muslims left Arabia and spread the language into many other countries, even as far away as Spain.

Arabic-speaking people use the same written script everywhere, but spoken Arabic is slightly different in each of the Arab countries.

Arabic is important, because the Koran – the Muslim Holy Book – is written in classical Arabic. Classical Arabic is older and more difficult than the Arabic used today.

Muslim children all over the world must learn to read the Arabic in the Koran, even if they are not Arab. Muslim prayers are all in Arabic. A man calls the people to prayer five times a day from the top of the minaret in the mosque.

10 The school day and the school year

The school year in Dubai starts in the middle of September and ends in the middle of May. The pupils go to school every day of the week except Friday, but only in the mornings.

There are just two long terms in the year, from mid-September to mid-January, and from February to mid-May. The summer holiday is very long because it is too hot for school work.

Time	Lesson/Activity
7.30 – 7.45 p.m.	Assembly
7.45 – 8.30 a.m.	P.E.
8.30 – 9.15 a.m.	Arabic
9.15 – 10.00 a.m.	Science
10.00 – 10.15 a.m.	Break
10.15 – 11.00 a.m.	English
11.00 – 11.45 a.m.	Maths
11.45 a.m. – 12.30 p.m.	Religion

The pupils enjoy the three-week holiday in January because the weather is cool then, and there is a chance of rain on one or two days.

The school day begins at 7.30a.m. The younger pupils finish lessons at 11.45a.m., and the older ones at 12.30p.m.

There is no school on Fridays, because this is the Muslim holy day.

A typical school day for 9 and 10 year olds.

A typical school day

The school day at Al Khawaneej Girls' School begins with an outdoor assembly. This is loud and happy. Some of the girls play musical instruments, and everyone sings the national anthem. It is called 'Eeshi Biladi' – 'Long live my country'.

Assembly.

Break-time.

The pupils in Grades 1, 2, and 3 have five lessons each school day. Grades 4 to 6 have an extra lesson, so that they can learn about their environment.

At break-time the pupils run their own shop. The older girls take turns to sell crisps, chocolate and soft drinks. Some girls have an early breakfast before they go to school – eggs, cheese, milk and fruit. Others take sandwiches in a lunch box to eat during the break.

School is fun

Muslim children do not usually go to mixed schools, so there are separate schools for boys and for girls. The girls in Al Khawaneej enjoy going to school. Before the Girls' School was built in 1986, girls in the village had to leave school at the age of nine and stay at home. Now they can study until they are eighteen.

The girls are taught to be well-behaved and neatly dressed at all times. They have a school uniform – a grey-green tunic and a white blouse. The older girls wear white trousers under the tunic and a white Muslim headscarf.

The children do exercises before classes begin each day. They also have P.E. lessons of gymnastics, volleyball, or dancing. They dress in trousers and baggy T-shirts for these lessons.

At the end of term the girls put on dancing displays for their parents. They wear frilly party dresses given to them by the school.

Library class.

The older girls enjoy lessons in cooking and sewing.

11 What the children eat

School finishes before lunch-time, so the pupils eat lunch at home with their families. Lunch is the main meal of the day. Everyone sits on the floor in a circle, and food is served from large trays.

Families normally eat together, but when there are guests the men usually eat on their own.

Families in al Khawaneej eat at about 1.30 pm when everyone is at home. Rice with meat, chicken or fish is served for the meal. Arab people are known for their hospitality. When there are many guests, a whole sheep or a young camel may be roasted.

After the main meal, people eat fresh fruit and dates, and drink Arabic coffee. Dates and camel's milk are a traditional part of the Bedu food. Both of these are full of goodness. Arabic coffee is served in small round cups which are refilled many times. You must shake your cup gently from side to side to show when you have had enough.

The holy month of Ramadan

Ramadan is a special holy month in the Muslim year, and during this month Muslims must not eat or drink from dawn till dusk. This is known as 'fasting'.

Muslims believe that the Koran was shown by Allah (God) to his prophet Mohammed during this month. By fasting, a Muslim purifies his body and mind. Children can fast from the age of seven.

At the exact time of sunset a Muslim breaks his fast by eating and drinking. That is why this meal is called 'breakfast'. The second meal is just before sunrise.

Children in Dubai love Ramadan. It is an exciting month when families visit each other late in the evening. School hours are shorter and children sometimes sleep all afternoon so that they can stay awake at night.

In Ramadan there are special types of food and delicious sweets.

It is important to pray during Ramadan. The Al Khawaneej children sometimes go to a big mosque near Dubai. There is a special room for women there too.

25

12 Out of school activities

Primary schools in Dubai finish before lunchtime, so there is no time for school clubs. The girls in Al Khawaneej spend their afternoons at home. At weekends there are sometimes family trips to the sea or to a park.

In the afternoons the girls stay at home. They do their homework and play computer games.

The boys often meet to play football, and from the age of ten they learn to drive cars in the sand dunes.

The boys look after the family's goats and donkeys.

At weekends families sometimes go to the seaside. The girls swim in their dresses.

⬆ At weekends the girls may go to a nearby park with their families.

Amongst Bedu families it is the custom for the girls to stay at home most of the time. When they do go out, they are always accompanied by their mothers or by their brothers.

Village girls seldom visit Dubai, except when they go with the other women of the family to the gold or cloth souks. A souk is a market-place full of small shops or stalls. Shopping for fresh food is mostly done by the men. They visit the fish, meat and vegetable markets in Dubai.

Whenever they go out, the women of Dubai cover their clothes with a traditional black, silky cloak called an abaya. The village women also cover their faces with a veil or a mask.

A wedding

An Arab wedding is always exciting. Most of the girls in Al Khawaneej marry someone from the village – perhaps even their own cousins. Celebrations last for three nights, and there is dancing and feasting. The younger girls are allowed to stay up and watch.

13 Festivals

2nd December is National Day in Dubai. There are also two Muslim festivals every year called 'Eid'. Boys and girls wear new clothes on these days and receive presents.

National Day

National Day started in 1971 when the seven Arab Emirates first joined together. Buildings in Dubai City are decorated with strings of coloured lights and there is traditional dancing. The girls in Al Khawaneej make flags at school and sing about their country.

⬆ On National Day there are special celebrations in Dubai.

On Fridays and on special holidays throughout the winter months camel-races take place. It is a great honour to win, and there are expensive prizes of money and four-wheel drive cars. People from all over Dubai watch the races.

⬆ The brothers and fathers of the Al Khawaneej girls go to the races to watch their camels take part.

The Eid festivals

Every Muslim child looks forward to the Eid festivals.

One Eid festival celebrates the end of the month of Ramadan. The Muslim year is lunar. This means that it follows the cycles of the moon. Ramadan ends only when the new moon is sighted. Canons are fired, and a three-day holiday begins.

The other important Eid festival marks the end of the Hajj. The Hajj is a pilgrimage to the holy city of Mecca in Saudi Arabia. Every Muslim should go on a Hajj once in his or her lifetime. Non-Muslims are forbidden to enter Mecca.

Eid festivals are family occasions.
Everyone wishes each other Eid Mubarak ('blessed festival').

Family visits at Eid are always fun because Arab families are usually large, sometimes with as many as ten children. The families in Al Khawaneej belong to the same Bedu qabeela or group. This means that most of the pupils at the Girls' School are related to one another as sisters, cousins, or even aunts!

14 School outings

The primary classes in Al Khawaneej enjoy school outings. All the girls go on at least five trips a year. A visit to the park or to the zoo is the girls' favourite outing.

⬆ A school trip to the city centre of Dubai.

Some of the school outings are educational. The girls might visit a dairy farm, or a factory where macaroni is made.

In Grade 1 the girls go on a tour of Dubai called 'Know your City'. They see the buildings, visit one of the modern hospitals, and play games in an amusement centre.

A trip to the city of Dubai is very exciting, but the girls would not like to live there. They prefer living in their desert village, where they know everyone, and where life is slow and peaceful.

Glossary

Air conditioning	Air conditioning is a way of cooling the inside of buildings by using machines which blow out cold, dry air.
Arabian peninsula	The Arabian peninsula is a large piece of land sticking out to the east of Africa and mostly surrounded by sea.
Bedu	Bedu are the people in Arab countries who have always lived in the desert areas.
Chemicals	A chemical is a powder, liquid or gas which changes or makes something else change when it is mixed or heated.
Condense	When water vapour condenses it turns back into liquid water.
Creek	A creek is a long, narrow stretch of water coming in from the sea.
Crude oil	Crude oil is oil that has come straight from the ground. It is untreated.
Desert	A desert is land which is so dry that not very much can grow in it. It is very often sandy.
Earth's crust	The earth's crust is the hard outside covering of the earth.
Evaporate	When water evaporates it turns into a gas called water vapour. Liquids evaporate when they are heated.
Fossil	A fossil is a dead plant or animal which has left its shape in a rock after being squashed under the ground for millions of years.
National anthem	Every country has its own special song about itself called a national anthem.
Mecca	Mecca is a city in Saudi Arabia which is the holiest place for Muslims. When they pray to God, Muslims must turn towards Mecca.
Minaret	A minaret is a tall tower attached to a mosque from which a cryer calls the people to prayer.
Mosque	A mosque is a Muslim place of worship.
Muslim	A Muslim is a person who believes in Allah (God) and Allah's special messenger who was called Mohamed.
Muslim headscarf	Muslim women and girls cover their hair with a white or coloured headscarf when they go outside.
Oasis	An oasis is a place in the desert where trees and plants grow.
Oil	Oil is a thick, greasy liquid which we get from animals or plants, or from under the ground. Olive oil and petrol are two kinds of oil.

Peninsula   A peninsula is a piece of land which sticks out into the sea and has water round most of it.

Pilgrimage   When you go on a long journey to a very holy place you go on a pilgrimage

Underground wells An underground well is a deep hole which is dug down to where there is water under the ground so that the water can be pumped up.

Wadi   A wadi is a dry river bed in the desert which only has water in it for a few weeks of the year when it rains.

Wellfield   A wellfield is a low place under the ground where all the rain water slowly collects after trickling through the earth. Wells are dug at this place.

Further Information

Books

The following five books are Butterfly Books
and are published by Librairie du Liban, Beirut 1989
Oil
Animals and Birds of the Desert
Plants and Flowers of the Desert
Oases
Farming the Desert

Finding out about Deserts, Usborne Publishing Ltd 1990

The Official Dubai Guide, Dubai Commerce and Tourism Promotion Board

Al Hilal Guide – Living and working in Dubai, Al Hilal Publ. Bahrain 1984

Oil by Norman Wyner, Longman Structural Readers 1972

Reader's Digest Family Guide to Nature, Reader's Digest 1984